Sports

Imitating

Life

Sports Imitating Life
Published 2012
McLane Publishing LLC

ISBN: 978-0-9886186-0-2
Library of Congress Control Number:
2012922391

Cover created by Ben Dixon, RedFyve Design

Printed in the United States of America

Dedicated to

my dedicated Mom

To him that watches, everything is revealed.

Italian Proverb

Table of Contents:

Intro 1

What makes a coach..........
       good, great, the best............................ 3
Practical thoughts
       daily, weekly, monthly, season 7

Get while the getting is good 13
Can't win it all on the first day 17
Graduating to coach 23
Inspire them to be their best 27
Delivering the message 33
End goals drive daily path 39
Fun AND focus 43
Killer instinct 47
Power of choice 53
Choosing greatness 57
Building credibility 61
Pride - doing it right from the start..................... 65
Repeatable successful 69
Integrity 73
Respect 77
Perspective 81
Self advocacy with intent 85
Failure 91
Pressure 95
Big Game? Don't sweat it 99
Filling the gap 103

Example:
Warm ups   109
Practice   110
Game lineup   111
Attendance and minutes summary 112
Other quotes   113

Intro

Over years of coaching and teaching, I begin to see overlap. Ideas and lessons that appeared in sports, classrooms and everyday life. This book describes a number of these lessons and ideas that continued to surface. Whether they appeared to me during an intense basketball game or a math tutoring sessions. These ideas are both defining and widely applicable.

This book is intended to be a guide. In my opinion, many of these ideas are at the root of teaching and leading improvement. You can read it cover to cover, or just a bit here and there. Each and every piece could be applied to different situations in different ways.

It is intended to illuminate a possible angle to take on a problem. You personally will find the best application for the situation.

The layout is intended to spacious. It includes extra space for you to write notes or thoughts throughout the book.

What makes a coach

A good coach ...

Is in charge: Being coach is not being a player

Clearly defines expectations: State what is expected simply, clearly and often

Is firm and has integrity: If you say it, it happens. If you say "everyone touch the line or we run again", that is what needs to happen. Your word needs to mean something to the players

Wants the players to do well for themselves and the team: At the very least, you as the coach want them to play well so you look good.

Gives strategy and information: The players can only execute the strategy if you deliver it to them

Doesn't mess it up by over managing: Players play, coaches coach. Guide them, but the players will decide the game, allow them to make plays in the game.

A great coach...

Does everything a good coach does and also...

Sees the players for who they can be: Not just what they offer right now, but what they could become

Gives the players information that teaches AND leads them to a deeper understanding: Giving them the basics and the end goal allows them to derive means to the end that will exceed your explanations

Generates opportunities for the team with inspiration and lineup combinations: As a coach, you can guide the psyche of the team, altering the lineups, combinations, formations and strategies can generate momentum

Creates a team first environment: The players know what the team is aiming for and choose to become part of it

The best coach...

Does everything a great coach does and also...

Inspires the players to want to do better: Help the players see what they can be and build their own drive

Helps them learn to focus: The ability to focus is like a muscle, it can be improved and it is subject to fatigue

Teaches repeatable success: The team and players understand the steps to succeed

Helps the players know themselves: The team experience has increased their ability to identify their own strengths and how that fits in with the group

Practical thoughts

Season:

Strategy: Simple is beautiful. Work to understand the essence of game on a individual and team level. Distill that essence into something simple; something easy to remember and has widespread application. For example, "Offensively we attack space"

Discipline and order: As the coach, you are in charge. You set the direction. You are not another player and not their friend. You can be friendly, but what you say, goes.

Deal with reality: The players will play their hardest. The leaders will lead. Players will be focused. These are the ideals. You must work in reality, adjust to meet the reality of the situation, quickly.

Winning: As the coach, the best you can do is teach them to put themselves in a position to win and inspire them to do it over and over. You decide the strategy, they decide the game. Teach repeatable success.

Monthly:

Written reflection/quiz: provide an opportunity for the players to write down what they remember and are getting from it all. As a coach, this is always helpful, and insightful, sometimes humorous and shocking.

Self reflection: Take the time to ask yourself about the season. Questions like 'What has worked for the team? What has not? What does the group need most from you as the coach?'. Answer without attacking, but honestly.

Weekly:

Games: The competition itself is the whole point. Preparing the players to be ready physically and psychologically is of utmost importance. The sooner they can get comfortable in game, the better.

Weekly notes and reminders: Weekly reminders (email/hard copy) to parents and players are great. They help keep the schedule at the forefront of thought and maintain open communication within the group

Daily:

Practice: Plain and simple, the point of practice is to prepare for competition. Everything during the time should be part of the plan to get ready, it should build towards the big goals of the season

Warmup: This provides a time for the players to get physically and mentally ready. Different teams need different warmups, but some kind of regular warmup provides function and structure for every team.

Project your voice without emotion: You as the coach need your players to hear your voice and instructions. If you scream with frantic anger in your voice, that's what they feel. Be loud without sounding angry. Deliver information, not emotion.

"Something good that someone did today": Allow a chance for players to compliment other players. It builds awareness and positive team spirit

1

Get while the getting is good

The beginning is the most important part of the work.

Plato

The blissful beginning of a relationship offers a limited opportunity. More specifically, every relationship starts with a "honeymoon" period; a time filled with optimism, energy and an effort to make a good impression. This period represents opportunity.

The beginning of the season is an opportunity of paramount importance. Setting the tone, establishing routine and kicking off a journey the hopefully ends with satisfaction. With a little intention on your part as the coach, the beginning of the relationship can set up for long term success, or as Bugs Bunny once said, "This looks like the beginning of a beautiful friendship."

One team that stands out in my mind was an 8th grade select basketball team. They were a wonderful group to work with, talented and willing. I vividly remember my 'tryout' practice under the eyes of a few involved parents. Upon calling the boys into the first huddle, they were silent; didn't whisper a word and were fully attentive. I used that time to talk about my expectations of their respect, effort and being a member of the team. I was as clear and firm as I could be in describing these expectations.

The season was a booming success. Both in terms of win-loss and the experience for everyone involved. The boys grew more comfortable with me and vice-versa. There would be times we'd make a joke in huddle, lightly rib one another, even have fun drills to keep it enjoyable. The underlying respect, and success, was in large part due to the firm tone I set to start.

Clarity in expectations have immeasurable value, they give guidelines by which to make choices. The beginning of any relationship affords you an opportunity to set these expectations, to mold what it will look like. Make use of this window and set the season up for success. Don't let this opportunity unknowingly pass you by.

2

Can't win it all on the first day

Coming together is a beginning;
keeping together is progress;
working together is success.

Henry Ford

Starting a season is much like starting a new job, friendship or even exercise routine. What will it look like on a daily basis? What kind of investment will it require to reach the desired goal? Most importantly, what are the steps along the way to get there? It's easy to be excited about something early. That eagerness and energy is great, but must be tempered with a realistic longterm plan in mind.

Starting strong is undeniably important, including setting the tone immediately. In essence saying, 'This is how it's going to be', right off the bat. Showing everyone involved that you, and your team, have an end goal, and a matching drive to reach it. There is huge value in starting with a determined mindset.

This 'start' must be tempered with a realistic mindset. Just as the team can't score enough points in the first quarter to guarantee winning the season championship, the team can't win it all in the first week. No singular expenditure of energy in the beginning will guarantee success later.

The expectations have to be set by the end goal, but leave room for reality. If winning the championship is the end goal, the first practice should include talk of that. It should also include talk that this will come with hours of work, but also challenges and setbacks along the way; lost games, injured players, embarrassing mistakes, emotional ups and downs are inevitable.

These bumps in the road don't mean failure, merely a foreseeable obstacle.

To set an expectation of an undefeated season is a perfect example of a goal that will be hard on the group. Is it extremely difficult to deliver, but most importantly, what happens if the team losses? The whole year can be deemed a failure. The group suffers an emotional blow. Whether they are mad at others or mad at themselves, credibility has been lost. Those that had invested in the goal, will feel less 'buy in'. The resulting spirit and performance will certainly take a down turn.

Set the tone firmly from the beginning. Have a realistic set of goals and know it will be a long journey filled with lots of work. A good beginning is a great way to start the season, but there is plenty of work ahead.

3

Graduating to coach

*A genuine leader is not a searcher
for consensus but a molder of
consensus.*
Martin Luther King, Jr.

As a young coach, it's hard to move into the new authoritative state of mind. Usually you have interest in being a coach because playing was enjoyable. It was fun to be with the teammates, it was fun to be part of the team, it was fun to play. Coaches can have fun too, but it's not the same type of fun because your are now in charge.

As the coach, it is imperative to have a delineation between the players and yourself. Regardless of how young, fun loving or accomplished a player you are. The coach is in charge. The coach's actions dictate the overall direction and attitude of the team. Creating that system doesn't allow for the same jovial camaraderie of being a player.

It can be a hard transition. One of

the hardest parts lies in how the players treat you. As a coach they are likely to treat you well. The players treat you (the coach) in a way that desires your attention, as if you are popular, important, even cool. It feels similar to being the star player.

To truly be an effective leader, you can't be "one of the guys". Establishing the system and direction for the team is of primary importance.

This doesn't necessarily translate into being cruel to the players. Nor does it mean you have to be perceived in a negative way. Effective coaches treat their players with respect, help them feel like, and be, part of the group. All of these are doable without presenting in a raging, screaming, demoralizing and/or crushing way.

Balancing being in charge with civil interactions is doable. You can create a friendly and kind relationship with the team and your players, but you are not their friend and they are not your equal.

4

Inspire them to be their best

If your actions inspire others to dream more, learn more, do more and become more, you are a leader.

John Quincy Adams

With respect to viewing players, there are two extremes. At one end, the players are seen as set pieces, they bring a given and unchanging value to the team. In essence they are a cog in the machine, they bring certain abilities that are categorical and fit somewhere in the team structure.

At the other end, lies a view that each and every player is an individual that has yet to reach their potential. Each and every one of them has leaps and bounds worth of improvement in front of them. They can reach a new level. Seeing each player as the best they could possibly be.

Finding a balance between these two helps the entire team. The strategy should be based on the reality of the situation, all the while keeping the potential in mind.

Over the course of a season, the player will improve simply by competing and participating. The practice and experience will lead to more efficient and effective play. This improvement can be significantly bolstered by a coach that is willing to invest time in directing the players' progression and growth. This can take many forms, but at the heart is the belief the player can improve.

If the coach believes the player can improve, that belief permeates the interactions; it is an unspoken boost to the player and team.

Long term improvement must come from within the player. You as coach will provide some 'kick in the pants' correction and some encouraging correction, but they have to want to get better.

The best way to embed long term desire to improve comes from inspiration. One of the best things a coach can do is inspire the player to want to be better.

The inspiration can come from desire to be recognized, desire to be the best, desire to push oneself or simply competitive drive.

Inspiring them to want to become better, will provide a lasting change.

They will drive themselves to improve. They will WANT to be a better player. Teaching them to drive themselves is a gift to the player. A gift that will serve the team for this season and the player a lifetime.

5

Delivering the message

A coach is someone who can give correction without causing resentment.

John Wooden

Sometimes the best lessons come from screaming maniacs; sometimes they come from soft spoken wallflowers. Good advice can come at you anytime, especially if you can see past the tone. As a coach, you want the players to hear the message, not the emotion. This means being extremely mindful of your tone.

Everybody has a natural tone, a baseline manner in which they communicate. The emotion of a moment can shift that tone drastically. Having your message heard is more important than succumbing to the emotion of the moment.

Let's use watching a football game as an example. The camera will likely find one of the coaches that looks furious; he is shouting and screaming at the players. Within short order, you could see another that looks as cool as ice; he is calmly and coolly discussing or review something with players. Two coaches from the same team, delivering messages in opposite manners.

The team's goal remains the same, but the matter of delivery couldn't be more different. Both coaches have strategy crucial to the success of the team. Despite the difference in delivery, both coaches want their players to implement a certain strategy on the field; both want success.

As a coach, it's important to be aware of your tone with the players. This includes understanding how they are taking it in. Sometimes players (and teams, for that matter) need to hear it in a certain tone. Often times, changing your tone as a coach doesn't need to be a complete makeover, but rather a subtle shift. The change doesn't need to be from drill sergeant to librarian, or vice versa.

On the other hand, you could argue it is the players' responsibility to filter out the emotion and glean the relevant message. There is merit and value to this point of view. A useful skill, no doubt. However, in this case, the coach is setting the direction, standing on the sideline (rather than running around dealing with the immediacy of the game) and almost certainly the older of the two; I'm placing the responsibility on the coach.

Using a combination of experience and a little perspective, you might be able to tailor the message quickly and effectively. Your goal as a coach is to teach, the easier it is for the player to hear the lesson, the better the job you are doing

6

End goals drive daily path

Efforts and courage are not enough without purpose and direction.
John F. Kennedy

I remember a young coach once asking me about practices, "How do you organize your practices?". Based on the broadness of the question, I sensed they were feeling a little overwhelmed at the prospect of directing an entire season. Reflexively, I answered 'Well, everything in the practice is either fitness, technique or tactics. I just go from there."

Before that, I had never put my thoughts into such words, but realized I had been doing that for years. It is easy to get caught up in 'being a coach' and forgetting to let the players learn how to play. Your job as the coach is to prepare them for the games. More specifically, your job is to distill that preparation into a practice.

Planning the practice is a necessity. It allows you to have a direction, shows the players you are prepared and gives structure. It is the blueprint for what will be taught in the session, it is the guide.

A guide is meant to direct, not dictate. It's easy to get lost in the daily details. The practice timing, the drills, the amount of time spent on certain aspects of the game, etc. Planning the practice down to the second can create frustration on your part. All of those thing are secondary to progressing towards the end goal. The practice is meant to serve the end goal, it can be flexible.

Categorizing the type of drills into fitness, technique and tactics is one way of tracking how time is being spent. It can also serve as areas within which to have intermediate goals. The practice pieces can fit into one of those categories.

Having an end goal, an idea where you want to end up, can bring clarity and purpose to every day planning. Progress towards the goal is the most important measure of the time spent.

7

Fun AND focus

People rarely succeed unless they
have fun in what they are doing.
Dale Carnegie

How many times can we remember hearing "to stop goofing around and get to work"? Which raises the question, is it possible to have fun and progress towards your goal at the same time? Are the ideas of fun and focus mutually exclusive?

Combining the two is possible, especially when the task at hand is participating in a sport.

For this case, we'll define fun broadly as having a good time, enjoying the process and embodying a general levity in the situation. In other words, having fun with it.

Focus will be defined as making progress towards the end goal. Having noticeable improvement and clear progress to reach the destination. Also known as, getting it done.

These two states can be balanced. They do not need to be in contradiction, destined never to co-exist in the same moment. Sports provides a perfect place to mesh these two ideals. To enjoy doing your best, having satisfaction with the task, and all the while truly exerting yourself to be at your best.

As a coach, setting this tone will fall squarely on you. It will be a balancing act. Individually, we all have a natural leaning towards having a jolly old time or getting out the checklist and going down the line. However, the team, or group, will also have a natural leaning, which will need to be accounted for in the interactions. Your job as the coach is to provide the guidance the team needs.

Having fun and focus in the same practice, game or season is doable. Sports are fun. Having a good time while doing your best is a reachable reality. It requires balancing the the two ideas with a firm but friendly tone. Finding that balance can make the season a great experience for all.

8

Killer instinct

The successful warrior is the
average man, with laser-like focus

Bruce Lee

How many times do you see a
team race out to a big lead only to
slowly lose it? Eventually seeing the
game come down to a couple of plays.
Only now, the previously losing team
has all the momentum. Now they are

the ones to make the decisive plays in their favor. When it comes to these types of games, coaches and players talk about killer instinct. "They should have put them away, didn't finish them off, they had no killer instinct".

This definition is one version of killer instinct, but simply put, killer instinct is the ability to keep focus when it is easy to lose it.

Focus is simply actively paying attention and not getting distracted. It is being fully in the moment. It's easy to get distracted when you have a gigantic lead. It's easy to get distracted when you face a gigantic deficit. Either the other team seems helpless and your team can do no wrong, or vice versa. Piece of cake, consider it done, this one is in the bag.

But wait a minute... time passes, the lead remains unchanged and the players' focus starts to drift a bit. The losing team makes a few plays and builds a little momentum. Then they make a few more. Before you know it, they're back in the game, with the 'winning' team on their heels and searching for that same mojo that previously built the lead. As for the 'losing' team, they aren't just just back in the game, but back in the game AND they have the momentum!

Guiding your players to weather the big leads and the big deficits comes to the forefront in these type of situations. Going up big or down big is inevitable. Teaching the players that focus is part of the daily expectation helps to make it habit; a habit that will help them deal with these large score differences. As it becomes habit, it is easier to recall that state of being focused, regardless of the score at hand.

Focus is a skill that can be improved. It is a state of mind that can, and should, be practiced.

Maintaining focus allows them to

work through these ups and downs of the game and the season. It also gives them a fighting chance against these big differential games.

Killer instinct is their power to maintain the mental focus when everything around them encourages loosing it. Killer instinct means finishing what was started.

9

Power of choice

The function of education is to teach one to think intensively and to think critically. Intelligence plus character - that is the goal of true education.

Martin Luther King, Jr.

As a coach, you are limited in your impact on the game. In fact, none of your physical actions can directly impact the game; none of them. The ability to choose what to do and how to physically react to the game situations, lies squarely with your players.

Coaches will make choices that impact the game; the lineups, the words you use with players, the emotional tone of your interactions, the example you set, even your body language. You have a large impact on the game.

Your greatest impact will be made through the players. It will manifest by how you have taught the players to make choices within the strategy. Helping them internalize the framework will produce great rewards. You can teach them which choices to make, the power they hold, and by extension, you can impact the game through their choices.

After they realize the control they have, they can begin to implement your strategy. The players will execute your plan.

Choice is power. Just as the players have the choices that impact the game play, you as coach have the power to teach them and guide them towards certain decisions. You must teach them the strategy you want.

In addition to the teaching those choices, you control the game lineups. Whatever the situation is, you always have the power to choose how to react. Your choice can have an real impact on the outcome. A powerful idea, for coaches, players and anyone else.

10

Choosing

greatness

We are what we repeatedly do.
Excellence, then, is not an act, but
a habit.
Aristotle

Sports throw a lot at you, and acknowledging your choice is a great start. The choice of how to deal with it, however, will dictate the likely outcomes. How do you help your players make choices that help them excel? That help them not just deal with it, but make use of it? How do you help them become great?

Of course there is innate talent and ability, but choice plays a huge role in the path to greatness. I'm not just talking about waking up one morning and thinking 'I really want to be the best golfer of all time'. I'm talking about the commitment, determination and drive to be great. Being the best of all time is not within reach for many, but being the best they can be, being great in their own capacity, is within reach.

Having players say they want to be great, is a promising indication. But talk is cheap, saying you want to be great, or reach some fantastic goal is easy. For them to truly make that choice means making a commitment. It means finding motivation from within. It means maintaining that determination over time. It means making the choice time and time again, becoming great is a habit.

For example becoming a great scorer in basketball is a goal of many young players. Desiring this status and recognition is step one of many. To truly become great at scoring requires hours of dribbling, shooting, practicing moves and playing. This player has the beginnings, the desire to be great. As a coach you want to encourage this drive and inspire to take on the cost of becoming great.

In essence, reaching a life altering goal means making life altering choices all the time. Total buy in, complete and thorough commitment over and over. Bringing the determination to make the sacrifices and do the work is the hallmark of someone on the path to success. Greatness can be earned by choosing it over and over.

11

Building credibility

If you whoop and holler all the time, the players just get used to it.

Paul Bryant

Watching a game, you see it all the time, a bang-bang play happens, forcing the official to make the call and it goes in favor of the 'superstar' and against the 'no-name', or at least, the lesser thought of player. This is also known as, 'the superstar call'. The star player gets the benefit of the doubt when the official is forced to reacted quickly. This a living example of credibility.

Young players need help to understand the choices they make define their character and how others react to them. These choices result in building an image in others' minds.

The concept of credit is easily applicable to money. A company is willing to lend money to an individual based on their qualifications and past choices that have made. An identical process can be used for emotional and psychological credibility.

For example, a sports player that has been one of the hardest working and 'clean' playing (doesn't bend the rules) for years, will have likely earned a positive image in the referees eyes. The past performances have built a positive image. This reputation will increase the likelihood that the call will go in their favor.

Credibility has been built and cashed in on, without a word being spoken.

Helping your players see the long term results of their decisions is useful. It gets them thinking about little choices they make. The concept starts with the coach. If you hold petty grudges and consistently take it out on players, then the players both see and learn this. If you talk with them candidly and upfront, you create an environment of integrity and ownership. Creditability can't help but result that, whether it is with the refs or otherwise.

12

Pride – doing it right from the start

It is easier to build strong children
than to repair broken men.
Frederick Douglass

Pride has two very different connotations. The first of which is a positive thing, like when you talk about something you are proud of. For example 'I'm proud of that game we played!". It is usually a result of how much effort has been put into it. The satisfaction in knowing that this work could represent you. A stranger could see it and you would be proud to say it is a representative of you.

The other type of pride, is not so positive. It is usually used to describe a type of arrogance. This kind of pride is usually rooted in feeling superior; feeling as though you are better and above the same rules that apply to everyone else. In short, thinking you are too good.

The players on a team WANT to be proud, in a good way. They want to be part of a group. Engendering good pride can be a powerful state of mind for the team. It can create a feeling that everything they produce, could be a representative of them. Having them feel that the effort is worth it, because the team represents them and vice versa. This can drive them to put great effort into seemingly little moments. Important, because some of those moments, aren't so little.

The little things DO matter, especially in sports. When the players have pride in the process, these details are automatically accounted for. The beauty of building this kind of habit, is how it eventually becomes the norm. The diligence will become the underlying trait of the group. That diligence and effort will amplify the natural talents.

Eventually those innate talents become secondary to the definition of character, the icing on the cake so to speak. They will be known as not just skilled, but rather as relentless and skilled. Not just smart, but dependable and smart. They can become the one to count in. In other words, having pride can lead to becoming an indispensable member of the team.

13

Repeatable

success

Success is a science; if you have the conditions, you get the result.
Oscar Wilde

How do the best of the best win competitions over and over? What do they do to be in that position almost every time? Most coaches call those 'the little things' or 'the details'. Recognizing how those 'little things' decide the game, allow the players to be successful over and over.

All of these 'little things' are concepts that we've touched on. The idea of putting out your best effort, physically and psychologically. Having pride in each of the things you do. Demonstrating respect towards the competition, as well as all others involved.

One of the final keys lies in the idea of pattern recognition. The idea of seeing a situation, evaluating it, and applying your talents. Actively paying attention and choosing accordingly. The world's best athletes are fantastic at this.

Pattern recognition is defining to greatness.

So how do you get better at recognizing patterns? As a coach your task is to help players identify things to look for. You are to teach the players what to recognize and what decision should be made. It is your job to teach them the application of the strategy.

As players, it is their job to pay attention, do their best and evaluate the results. In practice, that requires that they actively take in the strategy. In the game, it requires their best physical and mental effort. They must take in the surroundings and situations.

One basketball play I remember demonstrates this concept. An opposing player got by our defender on the perimeter and thought he had a free path to the hoop. I saw one of our best athletes see the breakdown from the other side of the court. He started to move over for the block. I KNEW he would block the shot. Only a second latter, the opponent attempted to put up his layup up and it was forcefully blocked out of bounds. I recognized the pattern, my player recognized the pattern, but the opponent did not.

The ability to pay attention, to take in information and act accordingly sounds like common sense, but it is the definition of being a successful coach or player.

14

Integrity

*I meant what I said and I said
what I meant.*
Dr. Seuss

A match between what is said and
what is done, a unity of speech and
choice; in other words, integrity. Having
this match, is a pillar for having any
civilized interactions. On the practice
field, after the game or anywhere else
for that matter; having credence for
words is the basis for society.

As the coach, you will likely be dealing with younger people. Think back to your younger days. If your parents mentioned the possibility of a trip to the water park, that felt like a promise. Huge value was placed on the words alone. Just as importantly, great disappointment was felt if it didn't happen.

We have a similar responsibility to the team. Our words need to carry great integrity. What is said to them, needs to feel valuable. If you say everyone is expected to be on time or they do push ups, that is what needs to happen for everyone, every time. You are setting the tone and direction for the team, not making good on your own word tears at your own credibility. It ruins your ability to convince the players.

Players and coaches need to have an unspoken trust. A trust that means what is said, is what will happen.

Discrepancies between the things we pronounce and things we do, can seem minimal internally to us. "Surely the players understood that was just an expression" or "Of course they sensed the sarcasm". That perceived difference erodes the trust between players and coach.

Building credibility requires great diligence on your part. You must hold yourself to a 'perfect' standard. Not in the sense of always saying the correct thing, but in holding true to your statements and in following through. If you do, you will create great value on your words, which will spread to the team.

15

Respect

Without feelings of respect, what is there to distinguish men from beasts?
Confucius

We have all heard lots of sayings about respect; "You should respect you elders" and "You gotta give respect to get respect". Even Aretha Franklin made a hit song about it. But at the heart of it, respect is a simple idea, it comes down to recognizing and valuing other peoples' efforts.

Respect is a simple concept; acknowledgment of someone's efforts. Being able to put yourself in their shoes and see the effort they have invested. Then choosing to display value for that effort. Simple idea, but easier said than done.

The part that isn't always immediately obvious, is seeing their effort. Measuring someone else's effort is hard to do. There is no universal measurement of effort, so it becomes largely subjective. Regardless, most everyone wants to have their efforts recognized. Attempting to recognize someone else's effort, is the first step in having them do the same for you.

Pushing your players to see respect in this light goes a long way. The expectation of respect is no longer just an edict forced onto them, but rather a way of interacting with others. You as the coach recognize their effort, which sets the example for them attempting to do the same for others. They are now encouraged to interact in a similarly respectful and aware manner.

The idea of respect can take many forms; giving someone your attention while conversing, considering the advice from someone, being on time for a group or simply playing hard. All of these very specific examples are great to see in action. Helping the players gain a true understanding of respect will raise them above any individual rule for the team; it will elevate their humanity.

16

Perspective

Know thy self, know thy enemy. A thousand battles, a thousand victories.
Sun Tzu

Perspective is one of the truest forms of intelligence. It is the ability to see a situation from some point of view other than your own; the ability to consider other angles. It allows people to learn purely by observation. It allows people to become smarter, by act of simply taking in information and actively paying attention. Experience plays an immeasurable role in learning, however using this idea of perspective can greatly accelerate the learning curve.

The simplest form of using perspective is very fundamental; watch someone make a mistake with immediate negative feedback and internalize the lesson. It could be as elementary as the proverbial slap on the head after stealing from the cookie jar. See a mistake and the repercussions, and now you don't need to make it for yourself.

This applies for positive experiences as well. For example, watching a great orator give a speech and noticing some of their techniques, then adding them to your delivery. By noticing what works well for others and applying it to your own methods, you can become better simply by observing.

As a coach you NEED your players to be able to learn this way. It is impossible to practice every situation. The variations and nuances of playing the game are literally endless. Helping the players learn to take in the lessons and project strategy and ideas is necessary.

Actively paying attention and taking in information allows them to create a catalog of likely outcomes. This is at the heart of being an effective coach. The ability to put oneself in the players point of view is essential to teaching them. Once you have a sense of their point of view, the strategy and verbiage can be tailored to help them progress.

The ability to see and know a situation it in a different way is the heart of perspective. This ability is the core of effectively teaching and coaching. Whether using perspective to customize your lessons or teaching the players to use it, having another point of view is smart, a true mark of intelligence.

17

Self advocacy
with intent

If you can keep your wits about you while all others are losing theirs, and blaming you. The world will be yours and everything in it, what's more, you'll be a man, my son.

Rudyard Kipling

Maybe as a player, maybe as a coach, or maybe as a spectator, we've all seen it or been subject to it. The heat of the moment. The referee makes a bad call, and someone just LOSES it towards the ref. It is easy to fall into an emotional state and begin berating the refs. Unfortunately, by hollering at them, it does not serve your cause.

This concept of perspective focuses on seeing it from another person's point of view. If you yell at the ref, they are not inclined to see it from you perspective. Your motivation is to have an even and fair application of the rules.

Self advocacy is a skill. It can be learned and improved on. First things first, what is the motivation? You (as the person requesting) have one goal and that is to get the decision maker to see your point of view. One quick way to ruin this, is to come at them aggressively and accusatorily. By throwing blame around and acting as if they have wronged you; it pushes your goal farther away. It's important to remember that they hold the power in this specific situation. Your best hope is to get them to see your point of view and empathize with it.

As a coach, it's easy to get emotionally wrapped up in the moment and holler at the refs immediately. The fact is, you'd be better serverd to wait for a break in the action and calmly call their attention to point of contention. Even better if you can do this after an obvious infraction has occurred. This approach shows respect. By doing it a manner that is not blaming, it gives them a chance to save face and to make the correct call next time. It also shows you know they blew it and still choose to maintain civility.

You leave the opportunity for the other person to own the mistake and move on without negative emotion.

On the flip side, it you choose to berate them, you likely make them feel guilty, or worse, justified. If this happens, they don't want to help you, instead they want to get back with whatever power they have.

All you want is a fair game. One that is decided by the players, not the officials or the opponent's abuse of the rules. You want a game that is decided by the players' skills and abilities; that is your motivation, that is what you want the refs to do for you.

18

Failure

Our greatest glory is not in never failing, but in rising up every time we fail.

Ralph Waldo Emerson

It takes a lot of effort and little luck to be great at something. Heck, it takes a lot just to be pretty good. A big piece of reaching such competency includes a willingness to fail. Mistakes are inevitable. Perfection is a goal to strive for, but will only be accomplished momentarily. Helping the players accept that mistakes are part of existence, is primary for them to reach their full potential. If they are consumed with worry, concern of 'looking bad', they will never reach their potential. They will always be wary of putting out their best effort, held back by a fear of failing.

Accepting these inevitable failures and short comings needs to become a secondary worry; secondary to not putting out their best effort. The players must be willing to have failures. As the coach, you can help them by recognizing which mistakes are results of inexperience and which are unacceptable lapses of judgment.

Help the players know their limits. The better they know their abilities, the easier it is to play the game accordingly. If a player knows that they are strong on defense, that knowledge will build confidence. That confidence can push them to play even harder and take more risks, further pushing the limits of their experience.

The past performances have been confidence building, so they know that putting out effort will likely result in a favorable outcome.

On the flip side, if they really struggle early, they are unlikely to make bold and decisive plays in the game. They become more timid and their play slips even further. Their worry of looking bad is causing them to be dominated and not just look bad, to be completely over matched emotionally.

The attitude to make assertive plays (or lack thereof) becomes a compounding cycle of reinforcement.

Coaches can help build knowledge of self in the players. Allowing mistakes is step one. Encouraging them to play hard while stretching their limits AND allowing them to move on from mistakes. Those experiences, whether embarrassing or confidence boosting, can help them expand their knowledge. Expect them to play their hardest, allow mistakes and move on; that will help them.

19

Pressure

The only pressure I'm under is the
pressure I've put on myself.

Mark Messier

When the game is on the line, the
heart beats a little faster, things feel a
little more anxious; everyone can feel
the pressure. The idea of pressure is an
interesting concept. The value of the
moment creates an increased feeling of

worry and possible failure. The physical task at hand has not changed, but the emotional environment has.

Helping the players understand and prepare for this is a good start. Start with the most obvious; they are doing something they've practiced many times, this situation is not physically new to them. Whether it is giving a speech, or making a free throw, it has been rehearsed. The task is unchanged, the same physical competency exists and they are just as good as they were in previous situations.

The mental aspect has changed, largely because of the weight of the outcome. Help them accept that it will feel different, but know that whatever competency exists, it is still there. Over time, they can and should feel confident in their usual ability. Part of the "been there before" benefit, is simply having experienced the feeling and being more comfortable with it.

As far as getting more comfortable in the moment. Help them relax. Reassure them. Take a minute to have them focus on what they can control. Very importantly, present a collected demeanor to them.

One way to alleviate the pressure is by using mental rehearsal and visualization. Before hand, spend time imagining the events unfold in a satisfactory way. Preparing your mind for the decisions, actions and mental state that will happen. For example, before a championship game, imagine your self making strong plays on defense, good passes to teammates, etc.. The more specific and true to life the rehearsal is in your mind, the more likely it will feel familiar and comfortable in real life.

Pressure is unavoidable, but understanding the parts that comprise pressure, make it manageable. Remember, most importantly, the physical abilities have not changed, despite the emotional difference.

20

Big game? Don't sweat it, just do what you do

Just play. Have fun. Enjoy the game.

Michael Jordan

As I've said, your primary job as coach it to teach them repeatable success, inspire them to do their best and provide a structure for the team. The championship game offers great notoriety for you as the coach. Unfortunately you don't have more control than a normal game. As important as it is for the coach, the best you can do prepare them to do their best, to set them up for success that THEY will seize.

In one sense, it's just another game. The outcome is of higher value, no doubt, but the physical motions and actions are identical to all the others. The game itself does not change. It is the same as all of the dozens of games leading up to it. It's for this reason that players should balance the 'big game mindset' with that of the normal mindset. As a player, to bring in a mindset of 'saving the world' or 'being the hero' simply adds pressure. Pressure that does not help individual performance.

Big game or not, players are well served to realistically set expectations. Have them ask themselves 'What does my normal good game look like? What kind of things do I normally do well?' Whatever they do best, help them focus on that. To expect a huge variation in the positive or negative respect, is foolish.

Help the player know what they are good at. Help them have a true and real evaluation of themselves. Help know that any given game could be their best, but regardless of the "quality" of their play, you expect them to do their best.

Big games can be more nerve wracking for the coach than for the players. You will be unable to make plays or physically effect the outcome. By helping your players have realistic expectations, they are likely to play a good game, even if it is season determining.

21

Filling the gap

Anytime you suffer a setback or disappointment, put your head down and plow ahead.

Les Brown

Over the course of the book, we've focused on being the coach. One aspect of being the coach is the physical removal from the game. The fact that the players must decide the game;

coaches are physically removed from impacting the game. This concept applies to dealing with emotional letdowns as well. Your players are destined for emotional disappointments. But just as a coach is removed from physically helping the team in game, you will be removed from directly coping with the players' letdown.

Your players will experience disappointment. Maybe a player hopes to lead the team in scoring. Maybe to be the best in the league or the best ever. Or maybe just to make an appearance in a game. Some level of disappointment is coming. Filling that gap between hopes and reality is no small feat. All of life is filled with things falling short of the dream.

Dealing with disappointment and letdowns are character defining. How they move on from the disappointment is a choice they must make. Making a certain type of decision time and time again moves it closer to becoming a habit. You as coach can guide them to positively deal with disappointment.

Coaches can encourage, enlighten, teach, guide and bolster their players. All of this helps them to prepare for letdown.

That gap between the dream and reality, can't be fixed or filled by anyone else; it has to be something they consciously choose to overcome. Finding a distraction can call focus away from it, but can't answer the question of how they can be satisfied with who they are after a loss. That lies squarely within their responsibility.

The letdowns are inevitable, but the choice of how to deal with it lies with the individual. You as coach can help them 'fill the gap', but just as they will ultimately decide the game, they will ultimately decide how to deal.

Don't cry because it's over.

Smile because it happened.

Dr. Seuss

Possible warm up exercises:

Toes – walking or jogging
Heels – walking or jogging
Lunges
Sideways lunge/groin stretch
Knee high run
Butt kick run
Superman (run with arms above head)
Slide (lateral slide with hips low)
Grapevine (lateral run, alternating trail leg in front of body and behind)
Slide recover (two slides, turn hips and sprint 2-3 steps, two slides)
1 leg balance (1-2-3-straight leg in front high as waist-swing to lift straight leg high as waist in back and touch ground)
Somersaults
Skip for height
Skip for distance
Backpedal
Back pedal with partner (match speed)
Backwards skip
Backwards long stride
Speed skaters (side to side bounding)
Two footed jumps/broad jumps
360 runs (as running spin a 360 with 2-3 steps)
Up downs (push up-> 2 foot jump, take 3 steps in between)
Piggy back race

Example practice plan

5	Talk – review game, getting to ball
~5-10	Warm up – extra backpedal
10	Short-short-long - step to the ball
10	First to the ball → attack goal
10	Run/races ?(relays, with ball)
~20	Scrimmage – first to the ball

	Talk – next game
	      something good someone else
	      did (put ups)

Example game lineup

Having the minutes played is useful. It can be a simple sheet, for this example:

Hank 14
Kurt 6
Jack 6
Nikolai 8
Josh 6
Carson 8
Billy 12
Jord 14
Kai 6
JB 8
Ian 6
Taylor 6

6	Kurt	Josh		Taylor	Ian
12		↑	Billy		↑
14		Nikolai			JB
		↑	↑	↑	↑
20:00	Hank	Jack	Carson	Jord	Kai

Example attendance and minutes summary

Last Name	Practices	Games	Minutes
Paulson	17	9	503
Martinson	17	9	473
Wrightson	14	9	470.5
Pearson	14	9	397.5
Markson	16	8	359.5
Martinson	15	7	348.5
Colson	14	9	336
Bilson	16	7	313.5
Smithson	16	7	310.5
Johnson	18	8	291.5
Robson	12	9	287
Lynnson	15	7	212.5
Tolson	10	7	191.5
Bryson	14	7	185.5
Jackson	11	8	175

Quotes:

There is only one corner of the universe you can be certain of improving, and that's your own self.
Aldous Huxley

The infinitely little have a pride infinitely great.
Voltaire

To expect the unexpected shows a thoroughly modern intellect.
Oscar Wilde

Perfection is not attainable, but if we chase perfection we can catch excellence.
Vince Lombardi

I never wanted to be the next Bruce Lee. I just wanted to be the first Jackie Chan.
Jackie Chan

There's no use fussing on a boy who doesn't have any ability.
Paul Bryant

It's kind of fun to do the impossible.
Walt Disney

You can observe a lot by just watching.
Yogi Berra

www.ingramcontent.com/pod-product-compliance
Lightning Source LLC
Chambersburg PA
CBHW070107070426
42448CB00038B/1842